That Which Is Everlasting

That Which Is Everlasting

Poems by

Kyle Singh

Cover image by Paul Gauguin *Animal Studies,* courtesy
of the National Gallery of Art Public Domain Images
Author photo courtesy of the author
Cover design by Shay Culligan

ISBN: 978-1-63980-473-3

Kelsay Books
502 South 1040 East, A-119
American Fork, Utah 84003
Kelsaybooks.com

Acknowledgments

I am tremendously grateful to the editors of the following publications in which the following poems, or earlier versions of them, first appeared.

Bloodroot: "A Theory on the Origin of Timber"

Clamantis: "Homebound," "Yew," "Moving In"

Literary Yard: "Brother," "Regressions"

NiftyLit: "To My Caretaker"

The Stonefence Review: "I, the Leafcutter Ant"

Straylight Literary Magazine: "Afraid to Ask You"

Young Ravens Literary Review: "A New Fawn"

Contents

What we cannot speak about we must pass over in silence.
—Wittgenstein

To My Caretaker

Am I gone now?
I asked you to tell me, say it was so
Did I remember who I was?
Had I somehow remembered where I had been
And what was to be made of the Coyote on the peak of the
    mountain?
The one that longed for remoteness
In the face of the hunt which was to come?

Did the lilies tell me how they stay afloat?
They swim against the current of my body
And fill my lungs with water
Where was I to go?
Moving through the sand
Shaken by the idleness of crabgrass

Before I thought of you as my own, did I meet you?
Was it you I saw on the lake wandering?

Somewhere, I have gathered a pile of land from where I have lived
And stored it for you to find.

Homebound

didn't you tell me, maybe I overheard you say,
you've kept soil from the spot you died

the nightstand near the window: legless
the window: breaks itself

bitter gourd with ridges, wedges it misses
dry air, ridges, make it miss when it was a whippersnapper

amalgam of millet, cumin, turmeric
amalgam of ash like a crinkled fly's wing

the integral substance is changing all the time
changing so it's not integral

extend torso to the door
roll up to the entrance with hands toward sky

make yourself soft and full: ovine
I meant to call you by a nickname

fingerprints on a doorknob
same as fingerprints on a moving train

suddenly sphinx can mingle again
suddenly I am cautious to look

Brother

You weren't yourself or really yet slouched over,
just a little lost for words, your unwashed face caught
within a small amount of doubt, which turned you
back into a man, someone—I guess—with wisdom.

I never quite got to know you, but I knew we would always
be interlocked, even in my dreams—or was it just hallucination—
It was almost as if we were trying to meet again
in the park hidden behind a dead end, broken swing sets,

sand always emptied out of the sandbox: that was the story
of why I chose to call, but even though we are siblings
I was shocked into the idea that we were symbiotic,
the physical stature of your posture: right beside me,

unshaven and stubbled, distant and still reciprocal.
Why is it so difficult, with you right next to me,
to feel like you'd rescue me from a burning building?
Why does your smile look so different from when

my hand touched your forehead as children? When I
saw you resign, reliable filled with warmth, it was clear
why we chose to travel across state lines, clarity of the bond
  –two broken in mitts—we knew not to embrace.

Forgive me. You came back when I asked you to leave,
so I could speak to you without forgetting that this back
and forth is a kind of shimmering. You will always be younger,
and still your forehead gleams. Run your car over the glove;

break it in.

A Theory on the Origin of Timber

Let it be, leave
the lid alone.
      I carry you
in a beechwood box,
hold you close to
let you forgive me.
It is a veil
which you inhabit;
your vision is
what calls me.
You are permanently
conceived as
the coarse grained
person in this
photograph.
      I carry you
in a beechwood box.
The smell of roots
is the way
the lid slides
off to reveal you.
All around you
in the foreground
are the things you
carried in your
hands—namely,
the mistake
of a jacket on
a humid day.
      I have sat you
upon velvet.
Reveal to me
what you were
born to, although
you were not
born

to the sensation
of falling into things,
stomping on each weed
rising upwards with
heavy sneakers.

This box was
my first project.
        I carved it and
whittled at it.
In this way
        I have become you,
as framed body.
        See how the patterns
in wood move
backwards and cross grained.
How they reminisce
In their random
decisions, how they
meet at the ends
and taper.
        I have not just made
this box-
        I have split the wood
with my ax. This is the origin
of timber. The ax is the start
of wood. Rosewood,
cypress, mahogany, spruce-
It is all the origin.
Yes, the origin
is an ending.
Your engraved
photo is ingrained
in this
beginning.

Now that I have come
to believe in
such legends,
       I must laminate
your image.

Moving In

Who will ask us to proclaim
that we are deadweight? Who will move
from the land of their past two generations
because that land is occupied by we who
are the first generation? There are no
remains from Byzantium, just
an unidentifiable patch
of swimming clouds. I remember
peeking out the window to check
if someone was looking. There was no
malt liquor for the masked jester
to rummage with his paws.
I remember trying to understand
the pact of neighbors, making
an offering of sweets to a mistaken
answer at the door.

First Spring

We had not known of silvery
Shadows and yet we had seen them
Stripped by the frost laid on the sheen
Of ice still slippery though it is March
How the frost is still laden
And fractured by the waxing
And the waning of whatever is answered
And forced upon beyond
What needs to be answered
We can only skate and run at the same time
When it is time to stop I cannot stop
When it is time to break I am still slipping
Sound of the voice of the one
I was supposed to meet
Oh, to slip in the clearing now
In what is distinguished
By all the accidents
They are all that there is

Regressions

My adopted aunty—you know, the kind who calls you her son
Assails my genetics. And that grin she wears now might
Be her passing lives. The future that dispenses and dispenses
Within us. That binds us and binds us and moves us and
Moves us. She goes for a walk with me on the trails,
And stares. Once, a girl who spent one year on the summit
Of an unnamed mountain. A stubborn girl. Jet black hair.
I would've wanted to be around her all the time. She, my
Guide, and I would walk above a stretch of ruts. When she stopped
I stopped. From time to time
She would ask unanswerable questions,
"How many miracles have you seen in the last five days?"
I'd always answer with another question:
You've heard the myth of the tin can? The metal
Which could speak of the stamp embossed in its frame
Could yield a description of how it started as a single
Scaffolding, how sharp it felt to be bent into a cylinder
Sanded down to the sparks, forged? The myth
Was whether or not the can jumped off the line
When it saw thousands like itself, assembled and filled
With minestrone soup. I explain to aunty that my favorite
Assignment in second grade was when I was asked to
"Describe the process of an object being made . . ."
"Yes, I did feel rockness," she answered.
"And I regressed to rock in my last life," she answered,
A sage in her nineties. My first idea
Of how to live in the world came from those
Who have learned to deal with it; who have made
From their lives a series of things.

A Vision

Those that are walking
  with their heads down,
in the service of arrival
  are simply tragedies
from our planet.

The rivets in their foreheads
  from squints
to resolve what is ahead
  in the search
of some kind of throughline, they

ignore our positions.
  I'm sure we could
locate ourselves, when placed
  beside one another,
when placed in an open plot

of grass, we'd step forward
  to nowhere, step
in the middle of ellipsis,
  we'd glow and not need
to know the escape of a sigh

an expansion of the diaphragm
  and release.
Those that have passed on
  would still want
the mystery of the act,

while still having the knowledge
  that they'd be okay
at the very least,
  O, what they'd do
for someone to ask them

how they felt right before
	it happened. And I?
I would grieve
	for the disconnectedness
of my planet, for how we still would

run to nowhere in that field,
	in the gaseous overflow
of fog, we'd still keep walking,
	as beta fish hurl into glass
we'd still keep walking, earnestly

to nowhere. One day, possibly
	in Spring, when the gift
of fogless morning is chosen
	to be delivered, I'll
witness how some will stop their stride

and press their hands over their eyes.

After School

The miraculous colored days just before we would grow old
but could still assume enough agency to walk home
alone from the bus stop,
so that what we saw was not just taken at face value,
and the suburb was still alive, filled with everything
we've ever known—
although there were so many things we did not claim to know—
why adults passed each other so quickly.
Once a boy some years older
walked right passed me with earplugs;
the air was so pleasant in the sharp comfort of September,
and I thought
of how he was unable to hear my voice. I would like to walk
just as slowly now, with some kind of voice. And each
day after school we would meet with big boxes
of chalk, the dust making us cackle like chain smokers,
we'd draw our oracles on concrete until
our hands seared, so that when it was time to
go home
it was as if we had imparted our legacy,
turning backwards to see ash from the map,
traveling through the air.

Myself

I

The eminent flatlands drone
      A rise in elevation catches the eye and commands it
         It forces me to look back and notice
            The outskirts which call me to stop

It is at this moment I will find it
I will not be a hitchhiker then

      It will be time to say one final word
      It will be time to settle in that place

I will have a new career and make fabrics, each from the carcasses
of beech trees, I will make the sheets each day and carefully stitch
them, I will find a craft, I will find myself.

II

The self should be found with others
Or instead when one is completely alone

We can never be truly alone

III

It could just be the kind of thing
      Everyone says when they hear your name

         Like the uneasy feeling we get
            when we hear *that* person's name

Somehow the shift always happens

Not able to face myself, I cannot face it

I, The Leafcutter Ant

—The ants go marching one by one, hurrah, hurrah!

I, the leafcutter ant, come with the Pharaoh and the Whitefooted one.

You've cupped your hands and made me dance, creator of patterns of light, you have guided me.

O, I am so grateful to you. O, silver headed God, thank you for this apple core, rotten and punctured.

Thank you for the dirt in the yard for me to burrow in, for the softness of your fingertips so my mandibles can draw blood.

Thank you

We carried aphids on our backs, green and sweet, the aphids were ready to yellow the leaves.

The leaves thanked us

Then, gently, we tapped them with our antennae and asked for sap, to protect them from the midges and lacewings.

The aphids thanked us

We have exchanged gifts with you now, God. I bow down to you and you to me.

And then there are the lasers, red dots in darkness, followed by sounds of crackling, swooshing release of a firecracker, the lasers on them, the sound of rockets and lasers on them, where are the beams coming from?

Such wild noises that make me scurry in frenzy, now curious about the nibbed pattern of rubber above, tacky, which smashes the pharaoh. Then there is some kind of odorless oil that the whitefooted one steps in, stepping into another time, not returning.

I hope I have left you something in return

Closeness

If we were to stand
Cheek to cheek

We would not have
Forgotten the ground

The beings within topsoil
That latch onto us

Each moment
Underneath the mulch

They beg us
For closeness

Once the hornworm made it
Past the tomato leaves

Onto my shoulder
Bare in Summer

It stood with me
Cheek to cheek

A New Fawn

In its first year, it was laid to rest
The earth blessed it with its final ritual
Rights granted by the angels of the underground—
millipede, woodlice, fungi, all ready to greet her
to return her into dust borrowed from the sky,
a trail of light, and the arched valley of water.
On her spots still filled with heat were patterns of shadow
I walked to her to place one hand on her mane
Where the foxes had laid their prey around her
My other hand on the fallen trunk of an oak
That took some 400 years to fall
I felt the pulse on my hand still alive
Small white flowers rose tall in the grove ahead

To Befriend a Cow

I sat upon the plot where
The cattle grazed, like urchins,
Each landing a lacquered tongue
Onto blade of grass
Tame, the mouths moved
Side to side and up around
How that repetitive motion
Hooked me on to them to watch
There, the plot stood at an altitude
For me to see them closely.
How often we are so far away.

Seasons had past with less to see,
Now the scalding heat
Of summer would hold itself out
Crop to fade, land not ready to harvest.

The rancher appeared then
In frenzy, more often than not,
He ran around in circles, he shook the heard
And rotated them out of sight,
Reinforcements for the land
That was once not dry
And was now drying out.

Because my intention was only to witness:
I was asked to leave and never return

Old Dog

Old dog, I have made you old
and turned your lemony coat white.

Old dog, I just can't help it
you should really just be with other dogs.

Your eyes meeting mine, mine meeting yours,
then turning them away, I from yours.
I can not look into them for long.

I, with nothing to give you
but guilt, and you giving gladness.

Old dog, I am sure you already know
when it is that you will die.

Old dog, I will not miss you.

I will understand that the Earth
has turned you into the scarlet streaking of morning,
or perhaps the chickadees limber penciled bill.

Yes, I will say this to myself,
I will say this to myself.

Dancing Man

Somewhere, I caught the breath
Of smoke, in grieving, each shard
Captured in the fickle way his bones
Dangled in his arms, each time he
Moved them each which way he moved
Them, he began to breathe heavier
The ash swelled on his lungs, it lit the
Linear form of his hair as it rolled itself
Down to his knees and up back to his neck

Some years later, now tied up in a bun
And some years after that, one lock
Now kept in a ziplock bag
Hidden from the sweat that dripped
Across his barren head, he flailed
Each arm with the same speed he did
Then, with each bop of his head,
He rocked like a chick as it knocks
Itself out of its shell

Inside Out

I

Absolutes call. They are punctuated and able.
Cherries still frozen refuse to thaw and make air thick.
Pigeons peck at each bushel, their rich
and pearly beaks fracture, hewn by shells of ice.
Poppy cones litter beneath ambushed fruit; it is winter.
The appendages are removed; a separation.

Wild in frenzy, they lumber and pucker their lips,
        (When you lost your beak were you left with lip?)
for the first time they are punctured yet able.
They refuse to stare down at remains that make dirt thick.
One moment before, a flock with pearly beaks, now it is winter.
        (Returned to squab have you become my friend?)

II

        All I want to say
Of the pigeons
Is that in their
Dismemberment
I finally saw them
As my own
        And yet
They want nothing
To do with me, how
They must be waddling as
Lazy eyed travelers
        I have squawked
For three weeks straight,
Puffed out my chest
By their nest,
        And yet, they
Have not appeared

III

Draw me to watch you like I have been chosen

This is a change of tense-

      The birds can notice,
now notice wilderness, they are wilderness.

The whole landscape can be seen,
         when it is turned inside out.

My skin is a dragonfly's

      Internal bones are exo

Interrupt me now

      Let me stay as I am

Don't make me possess

      How we always want

To possess

      Our bodies

IV

The winter is gone, the cherries are glowing,
each has fallen from foothills on pasture, off
of boughs they once sat on as cherries,
as cherries, as cherries, though the squirrels
found them as rubies, darker than the scarlet

of their assumed identity, a bounty of apples
instead, harsh, sour, out of season, waiting
for autumn, they plunge cores onto teeth.

V

All that has been given to me has never really been given. I have
been given this body, but this body is not mine. One day as a boy I
had decided to kill the earthworm, to take away life that had
somehow been given. As I began to push the flesh against my
wrist, I remembered that the act of being alive was not decided
upon but had to have been, for how else did the worm's interior
pulse faster, forcing me to release it into the lawn underfoot. Why
did the worm trek back into soil, right after, with indifference?

VI

Rupture
        my
                ribcage

Throw
        my
                fossil

Onto
        a
                hearth

Yew

I

The hallway beyond her room is narrowed
to a point, sill after sill are flower pots in terracotta
which hold plastic tulips and marigolds;
a watering can of play doh beside them. She is
a downy cheek as a pointillist collection of wrinkles.
When you sit next to her and listen, actually listen,
she leans in as if a secret fortune had been discovered.

An audience is finally present to hear a declaration
of how the lutefisk is too cold and how it was *de rigueur*
for the nurses to ask how each morning was treating her.
She looks right at you and makes you
look at the floor. In the squalor, a recognition
of unassuming eventfulness far from any elemental surprise.

But then there are times, her eyes flicker to
a rapid blinking as if blinking was voluntary,
as if she were haunted.
She turns away, she can't continue to look
right at you. And then a strange fall in the pitch of her voice
and that lanky jawline suffuses with color, overtaken
by a dream to correspond with an absence, an absence
of facility, an absence of where the room is.

She calculates how long it will take for her to know
and pass down what she learned as a child.

It is painfully beautiful: To watch someone become a new thing.
She is bereaved of all identifiers, she leans back
in her rocking chair and tells me her name is *Yew,*

tells me to remove each needle from her twigs
tells me to rid her of the poisonous berries she carries.
I'd like to ask her how I can carry out these wishes, when
dirt is what I'd like to keep separate from my shirt.

II

And yet the shrubs do not know that they will last forever, that
within them is pulp which could stain an entire lakeside, that their
visit for two weeks means I am certain to stand still. For two
weeks, I walk to you and gaze upon your branches. I am so distant,
you are still waiting; we come to meet each other but you cannot
understand. I live alone with myself, yet together with a spirit—a
drifter. I am immobile yet set to motion, persuaded by the illusion
that you have appeared before me as that spirit, an offering to
remain still. Now, I can never profess to understand how we can all
be part of the same light. On your supposed last day, when you
were about to turn from fruit back to flowers on strigs, I ripped you
from your bundles and threw you onto me, popped each husk onto
my arms, hurled them in a last attempt to become you. How the
juice of black currants became my entire arm. How the speckles of
violet washed into my hair.

Lakeside In Drought

I have begun the action
Of remembering again
The mind remembers to tell

Me of what it owns. Owns
What? Owns me.
I own nothing.

The things I love
Are below the surface
Of my reflection

The things I love
But have never seen
8-bits of code below

The boundary above the bulk
A hologram is the image
Gnats on the surface

Are what I can see on the surface

I can not see myself as whole
Unless I am completely still
And in reflection: the mirror.

The water, in front of you
The gnats are the open book
Stare closely and in stillness

Their wings vibrate violently
They perspire mist into the
Porous cavities of the ground

Can we taste-the sweat?
Have you finally remembered
The shape of the first
Creature you saw that was in
Freedom?

To drop the maze imprinted
Onto my fingerprints into
A clear surface, to submerge while

Forgetting that first creatures
Underbelly pulsating on the
curb, the underside of what

The mind remembers
Nothing to remember
But there is taste

In the acridness
Of water submerged in arm
Merged into arm hairs weighted

Both arms moving
Through water and now I am without
my arms, the rest of me

The rest of me still
On the surface, lakeside
Can I drink the water now?

Can I drink to remember
The sweetness of what
Sun can ripen until

It collapses on its own weight
Ripened until it does not
Need to remember

Until it completely filled
And can own a journey
From which it can not,

Need not, return

First Purpose

A goose leaves its migrating flock.

Its choice is no choice
of its own.

It says that its home,
a world not made of time,
has been conceived

out of intention, an animals
need to go screeching, soaring,

into a memory turned into
the present,

the animals treatise
of emblem and stillness,

the feathers which shed
and dispose of themselves.

A goose leaves the flock. Breaks
the sequence and shape
created in the sky,

settles into its nest,
where it was never to return,
a chick bare
in the street.

It is the purpose
arranged by all instincts,
what arranges inside an egg:
A warmer place for winter
is all that's missing.

Repentance in the beginning.
Repentance in the end.

That Which Is Everlasting

All speech, because it is river
and food, and gives us declaration,
what we believe in, identity, language
turns out to have never have happened,
except for when we are alone and it is between us,
between two interlinked inhabitants, visitors.
Look. I have called out my own name.
       The acknowledgement of wonder does
       fill our lives, our lives are not meaningless;
       you reaffirm this.
But don't expect, now,
to be remembered.
When I first realized that I had been given
a moment, I asked myself if I really needed it.
An undistinguished pit latches on to an empty stare;
small moths scuttle off the bark just as they did
in the last millenia.
       Try
to acknowledge the next moment as permanently
frozen, an undistinguished declaration, traversing
from end to end, experienced just once by
primal-originators in utter shock when
they were left without words.

Afraid to Ask You

Now that you are closer to me than I could have ever imagined
it is not love that I have come to

with its seeming dependencies and lack of impurity
still this fulfillment I cannot get rid of

still longing when there is nothing to long
flailing into the fact that you are still distant

thinking of asking you to take me in and dance
to no particular song

This.

I have fallen into excursions.

At one time it felt as if
        they were all that was;
This.
        let me succumb to a longing, dig into an identity.
You'd want one too?
        It is relaxed. It is a relaxed
moment, when light enters an eardrum and makes a sound,
an inflated plummeting of trills, cicadas carry a vesper,
double cover,
        at finite speed, double cover for the sound that
came a moment before it.

        This   is relegated

        To a location, a short trip to everything that
Sends a beam, a signal, trespasses aging, and yet

I am older.

Listen now:
        You speak one language that is not your own

What is it that makes me devoid of space?
        What will let me crowd my field of view

        Oh, mean spirited illusion, you know I want to be more
than a body
and yet how can a soul live in my gut.

"All moments are imitators of other moments"
"An affirmation is a continuation of an infinite series"
"I am a replica of a miniature figurine"

The figurine is sculpted by another body.
      It is not removed from it,
        yet it is inanimate, and I can still feel it.

Sour and curdled, sweet at the finish, spoon by spoonful
it is thrown
        into, the processor.

Do you remember forgetting the marsh you swelled in?
        Do you come to the tendrils in your garden as a deacon,
a carrier of prayer, sniper of will?

        I am willed to lift the bare trunk after stripping it
of all its bark. *Erode*
                 the tree.

A piece of rubber stretches to snap,
        as it lifts from the base to the husk.
This   is everything I can see, it snaps,

I am blinded. How physicality, can be, it
is, lightness.

About the Author

Kyle Singh is a graduate of the University of Pennsylvania where he studied theoretical physics and mathematics. He is currently a researcher on the foundations of Physics and Quantum Field Theory. At Dartmouth, he studied poetry with Cynthia Huntington. He has also translated the notable Punjabi poet Amrita Pritam. Several of his recent translations can be found in *ITERANT*. He is originally from New York.